Best College Match

Workbook

Gregory and Opal Dawson

Best College Match Workbook

Copyright © 2017 Gregory and Opal Dawson

All rights reserved. No part of this book may be reproduced, stored in a retrieval system, or transmitted by any means without the written permission of the author.

ISBN: 154412936X
ISBN-13: 978-1544129365

Printed in the United States of America

CONTENTS

1 **M**astering Personal Self Awareness — 7

2 **A**ccepting Ownership of Academic Competencies — 13

3 **T**houghtfully Identifying College Parameters — 23

4 **C**arefully Procuring College Funding — 33

5 **H**onestly Picking your Best College Match — 41

6 Addendum — 45

Gregory and Opal Dawson

Chapter 1   Mastering Personal Self-Awareness

As you transition to college it will serve you well to be totally honest with yourself about your own character. Knowing who you are, as a whole person, matters because it will take getting the best out of the "New You" to most successfully find your "Best College Match".

Identifying the "New You"

Use the Personal Profile chart below to determine your personal character type – please be honest with yourself as to who you really are *not* how others may perceive who you are.

Personal Profile
Commitment

	Lower	Higher
Responsibility — Higher	Place Holders	Rock Stars
Responsibility — Lower	Slackers	Up & Comers

The 4 Personal Character Types

Rock Stars are _____ students who are "in it to win it" as they are highly motivated, proactive and self-directed individuals who are highly engaged and highly involved in their personal self-development.

Place Holders are _____ students who are "going through the motions." They are poorly motivated, reactive, self-directed individuals who are less engaged, but still involved in their personal self-development.

Up & Comers are _____ students who are "works in progress." They are highly motivated, proactive, self-directed individuals who are highly engaged and poorly involved in their personal self-development.

Slackers are _____ students who are "entitled and self-centered." They are poorly motivated, reactive, self-directed individuals who are poorly engaged and poorly involved in their personal self-development.

My Personal Profile Type is most like that of a _____. Once you understand which Personal Profile Type you exhibit in your life then you can alter the aspects of yourself that are helping and hindering your progress towards the success you would have for your future.

Personal characteristics that help my success: _____

_____

_____

Things I can do to build on my successful characteristics: _____

_____

_____

Personal characteristics that hinder my success: _____

_____

_____

Things I can do to improve the characteristics that hinder my success: _____

_____

_____

Beyond simply understanding your Personal Profile, your ability to use it effectively requires that you be _____ with yourself because your personal character forms the _____ of your "Best College Match".

Remember . . .

> **"A winner is someone who recognizes his God-given talents, works his tail off to develop them into skills, and uses these skills to accomplish his goals".**
>
> - Larry Bird

So, now be prepared as the "New You" to _____ as we move forward to find your "Best College Match".

Begin with The End in Mind

To be most successful in finding and funding your "Best College Match" you will need to make your strongest possible applications to the colleges and or scholarships of your choice. Most of these applications will require much of the same information.

Therefore, to save time and create efficiency in developing strong college and scholarship applications, it is important to have as much of the application information prepared in advance as you can.

Action: Turn to the "Best College Match" Addendum at the end of this workbook and begin to complete the entire addendum as accurately, efficiently and fully as you can. Keep the completed information in a separate file as your personal "Best College Match War Chest" so that this application information can be referenced, tweaked and reused as needed throughout your application process.

Please do not skip this important part of the process. We are confident that preparing this information in advance will help you be more successful in finding and funding your "Best College Match". We used this same addendum and our son Blake won over $1,000,000 in merit based scholarships and a paid corporate internship. See Blake's Story at www.bestcollegematch.com

Who's Got My Back – Building A Strong BCM Home Team

Building a long-term, strong home, school, and community network of individuals to help support and guide your journey to find and fund your BCM is invaluable. Most adults, given a student's honest pursuit of furthering themselves, are almost always willing to provide support.

Therefore, build a strong team with individuals who really know you and can offer the highest level of tangible support that will help you the most when it's really needed. Adults, especially educational professionals, know those students who are sincere about their academic careers, and they have formed strong relationships with those students because of their dedication to their education.

Thus, these students, many of whom will need guidance, documentation, and letters of recommendation will generally get better, stronger, and faster support than those who do not have these great relationships. Including those who have not taken their school career as seriously as they should have before it was time to apply to college.

Teachers and school professionals are humans too, and they are keenly aware of their students' overall ability and sincerity through the college application and scholarship process.

So, seek the support of the types of people you will need when college application time begins. These adults have a lot of sway in either being a tremendous asset or yet another hurdle in your quest to obtain your Best College Match. If they are solidly on your team, they can offer very helpful suggestions, ideas, and resources to support you.

Applying for and winning admissions and scholarships is very competitive but with the support of your home team you'll find the process much easier.

Use the following BCM Home Team Document to build your own personal college support team.

BCM- Home Team Documentation

Student Name: _____

Parent / Guardian: _____

School Support

Teacher	email _____	phone _____
Counselor	email _____	phone _____
Principal	email _____	phone _____
Coach	email _____	phone _____

Non School Support

Program Director	email _____	phone _____
Non Profit	email _____	phone _____
Extra Curricular	email _____	phone _____
Church	email _____	phone _____
Mentor	email _____	phone _____
College Rep	email _____	phone _____
Alumni / Group	email _____	phone _____

Peer To Peer Support / "The Buddy System"

BCM student participants	email _____	phone _____
Classmates	email _____	phone _____

Chapter 2   Accepting Ownership of Academic Competencies

The students who are most successful at realizing their Best College Match are also most proficient in understanding and aligning their Academic Profile with the requirements needed to meet or exceed college and scholarship expectations.

Personal Competencies

Your Academic Profile quantifies your academic competency. The overall quality of your personal Academic Profile (record) will largely determine your most realistic future educational opportunities.

Colleges and scholarships utilize your Academic Profile (record) as the primary indicator of potential college success because they need to understand the overall strength of your educational background quickly.

Therefore, as part of the application process colleges and scholarships will almost always request a copy of your:
1. _____.
2. _____.

The fact is that colleges and scholarship committees use your Academic Profile to make (2) types of judgments about you which include:
1. _____ about your academic proficiency – the type of student you are.
2. _____ about your personal character – the type of person you are.

Academic Profile
Student Type

	Low	High
Performance High	**Casuals** (Under Motivated)	**Scholars** (High Achieving)
Performance Low	**Unprovens** (Unknown)	**Strivers** (Hardworking)

Ultimately, what colleges and scholarship committees really want to know about you is:

1. If you are the _____ of student that fits academically at their institution or scholarship.

2. If you are the _____ would enrich the value of their college or scholarship.

Your Academic Profile

Your Academic Profile consists of (2) very important interrelated parts that define your academic record as a student in relationship to:

1. The _____ of your record and the _____ of your classes including your ACT / SAT test scores.

2. Your _____ based the _____ you earned (your GPA) in those classes.

Best College Match Workbook

Making Your Academic Profile Work for You

To best increase the chances of finding and funding your "Best College Match," students MUST do (3) specific things to best utilize their own personal Academic Profile:

1. _____ It – your Academic Profile because you only get one.

2. _____ It – how your Academic Profile is used in determining future academic opportunities.

3. _____ It – your Academic Profile strategically based on admissions requirements (stay in your lane) because when you best _____, _____ and _____ your Academic Profile, you are best utilizing your own academic record to position yourself to achieve your greatest success.

Owning Your Academic Profile

Owning your Academic Profile (record) means making it work by understanding that:

1. It's based primarily on _____ and my _____.

2. Once it's completed, my record is_____.

3. It defines the general _____ of my college and scholarship opportunities.

4. It can be positively enhanced with additional supporting _____.

5. It's the _____ in comparing applicants for colleges and scholarships.

6. It must be strategically_____with my college and scholarship applications.

Charting My Personal Academic Record

Use the chart below to chart your own personal Academic Profile and see where your GPA and ACT/SAT Scores intersect:

My GPA_____.

My ACT/SAT Scores_____.

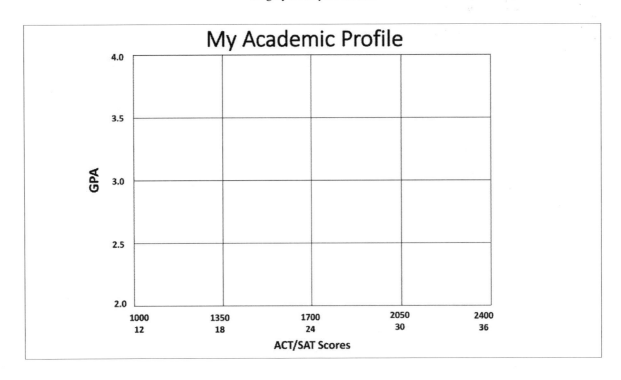

Understanding Your Academic Profile

Whatever your Academic Profile turns out to be, you will need to be _____ about it and _____ it with the colleges that are the most advantageous so that you can present yourself competitively to prospective colleges and earn the needed scholarships. Therefore, to find your "Best College Match," you must _____ your Academic Profile and seek to match it with the colleges that will _____.

The bottom line is to be the most successful in finding your "Best College Match" you need to be _____ and _____ about your Academic Profile and _____!

Align & Be Fine – Aligning Your Academic Profile for Success

To be consistently competitive throughout the application process **a smart rule of thumb is** – given your Academic Profile (your GPA and Scores) – _____ or _____ the average academic record among all applicants before the consideration of any additional supporting documentation.

Said another way, your Academic Profile should be generally between the _____ to _____ percentile of the colleges or scholarships general Application Profile for all applicants before any other considerations.

Don't Miss This! Aligning your Academic Profile in this manner is very important because it positions you for success by increasing your Relative Competitive Record as compared to the entire applicant pool.

Your_____is the comparison between how your personal Academic Profile compares to the Academic Profiles of all the applicants for admissions and or scholarships.

If your Academic Profile is higher than the average Academic Profile for that applicant pool, you will have a higher Relative Competitive Record and therefore increased chances for success versus if your Academic Profile is lower than the average Academic Profile for that applicant pool you will have a lower Relative Competitive Record and decreased chances of success.

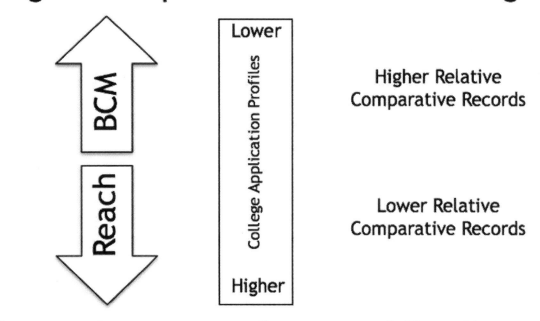

Note: Aligning your Academic Profile in the above manner makes your Relative Competitive Record immediately at least as good or better than average among all applicants within a given applicant pool which leads to higher admissions rates and greater funding packages.

How to Compare Relative Competitive Record (RCR)
Your ability to accurately compare your RCR against that of other applicants for admissions and scholarships quickly and efficiently will determine your success in finding and funding your "Best College Match".

Let's look at an example for our friend Joe whose Academic Profile consist of a 3.70 GPA and a 26 ACT.

Originally, Joe applied to a Reach University and was not accepted because his low Relative Comparative Record as compared to most other applicants with Academic Profiles averaging 3.89 GPA's and 30 ACTs resulted in the misalignment of Joe's Academic Profile with the larger applicant pool. Thus, given his desperately low Relative Competitive Record, Joe was out of his academic lane in applying to this college.

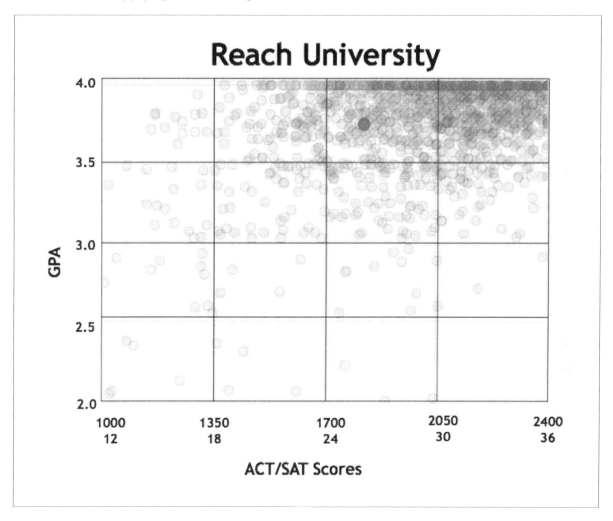

However, after Joe applied to a BCM University, he was accepted and won a strong funding package. His Relative Comparative Record as compared to most other applicants with Academic Profiles averaging 3.40 GPAs and 24 ACTs resulted in the strong alignment of Joe's Academic Profile as compared to the larger applicant pool. Thus, given his high Relative Comparative Record, Joe was totally in his academic lane in applying to this college.

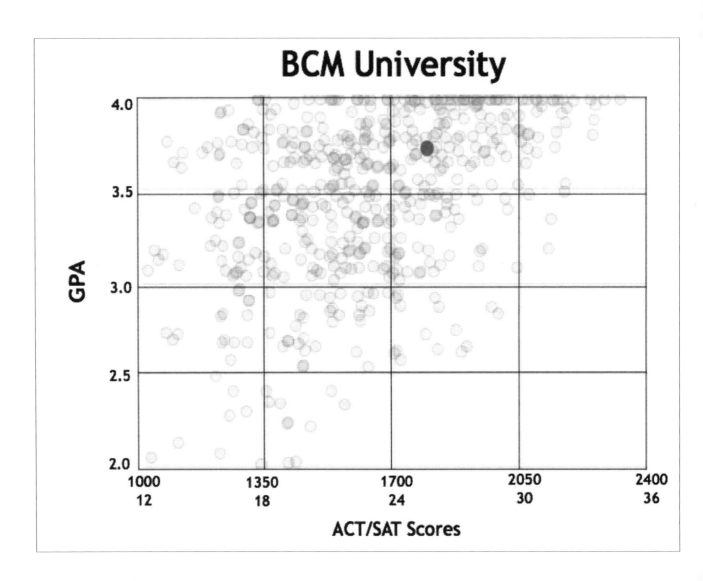

My Academic Profile Alignment

Place your Academic Profile scores both GPA and ACT / SAT in the Academic Profile chart. Use the average 50th Percentile as a starting point to look for colleges and or scholarships where your record will be at least competitive before any other special considerations.

GPA

25ᵗʰ Percentile _____   50ᵗʰ Percentile _____   75ᵗʰ Percentile _____

ACT / SAT

25ᵗʰ Percentile _____   50ᵗʰ Percentile _____   75ᵗʰ Percentile _____

Your Academic Profile = 50ᵗʰ Percentile (GPA & Scores)_____Alignment

Your Academic Profile > = 50ᵗʰ Percentile (GPA & Scores)_____Alignment

Your Academic Profile < 50ᵗʰ Percentile (GPA & Scores)_____Alignment

Lastly, your Academic Profile can be aligned at _____ or percentiles of the overall applicant pool to make your personal Relative Academic Record _____ or _____ competitive depending on your personal _____, _____ and _____.

Gregory and Opal Dawson

Chapter 3 Thoughtfully Identifying College Parameters

Choosing the right college to attend is one of the most important decisions you'll make. Therefore, when choosing your "Best College Match" consider colleges that are in your academic lane and that are personally agreeable in suiting your style as an individual.

Fit = _____ + _____.
     (_____) + (_____)

Identify colleges where you can feel totally free to grow as a student and a young adult.

Identifying Fit Colleges

In this section, you'll begin the process of identifying your "Best College Match" fits. This process can be fun, but fair warning, your end results will depend on how well you are able to identify colleges that are in your academic lane and also offer you the personal factors you would want in a college.

Remember your Academic Profile should be at least greater than or equal to 50% of each college or scholarships average applicant where when identifying your possible "Best College Match" you should follow the following steps.
1. Complete the My Personal College Factors worksheet to identify which of the 10 biggest Personal Factors are most important to you in finding your "Best College Match" fit.

My Personal College Factors

Major / Interest: (Offered)	Yes	No	
If Yes, List Major	_____		
Educational Quality:	Low	Medium	High
Admissions Selectivity:	Low	Medium	High
Financial Assistance:	Low	Medium	High
Retention & Graduation Rates:	Low	Medium	High
Type of Institution:	Public	Private	
Size:	Small	Medium	Large
Diversity & Demographics:	Low	Medium	High
Location:	Urban	Suburban	Rural
Close to Home:	Yes	No	

Intangibles

Prestige / Ranking:	High	Medium	Low
Study Abroad:	High	Medium	Low
Internships:	High	Medium	Low
Research Opportunities:	High	Medium	Low
Greek Life / Party Scene:	High	Medium	Low
Sports Inter / Intra:	High	Medium	Low
Other Personally Special:	High	Medium	Low
List: Other	High	Medium	Low

Action: Having completed the My Personal College Factors worksheet, please take the time to rank in order from highest to lowest priority your top 3 personal college factors.

1. _____
2. _____
3. _____

Be certain to keep all of your personal factors, especially your top 3, in mind as you search for personally compatible colleges.

1. Afterwards, research and identify 10 – 20 "Best College Match" possibilities, because many will fall off of your list as you narrow your choice. Have some fun and search widely even looking at colleges that you wouldn't think you'd normally consider. Developing a strong idea of what is available and what you like and dislike is important in finding your "Best College Match".

2. For completeness, consider a couple of strong preference schools where your Relative Comparative Record is upwards of 80% or 90% of the average as your *back-up colleges* as well as some that might be as low as 25% to 50% as your potential *dream college.* Also, add these types of colleges to your "Best College Match" list because there are no guarantees either way.

3. Once you're satisfied that you've identified strong "Best College Match" schools by accurately aligning your Academic Profile and your college personal factors enter your identified "Best College Match" schools on the following – My Personally Compatible Colleges form.

My Personally Compatible Colleges

1. _____
2. _____
3. _____
4. _____
5. _____
6. _____
7. _____
8. _____
9. _____
10. _____
11. _____
12. _____
13. _____
14. _____
15. _____
16. _____
17. _____
18. _____
19. _____
20. _____

4. The personally compatible "Best College Match" schools and/or scholarships should be the ones for which you apply, at a minimum. It has been our experience that as you are doing your research other college and scholarship opportunities will present themselves. We recommend that you apply for them as well.

This list of colleges you've just completed will now represent your baseline _____ as potential colleges that you feel would be both a great match for you_____ and _____.

The Four Types of College Fits

Based on your Relative Comparative Record and your own Personal Factors, your "Best College Match" schools will come in 4 types:

Specialty Fits are _____ and _____ colleges that offer a great fit based on a student's particular specialty or exceptional talent like athletic or artistic ability, debate prowess or even possibly a demographic group.

Highest Fits are _____ and _____ colleges that offer a great fit based on a student's exceptional academic merit and or complimentarily strong personal and academic resume.

Moderate Fits are _____ and _____ colleges that offer a good fit based on a student's solid academic and extracurricular record as compared to their general student applicant pool.

Selective Fits are _____ and _____ colleges that offer a good fit based on a student's very strong academic and personal record as compared to the general applicant pool at colleges in high-demand.

My "Best College Match" Type
Review the colleges listed on your My Personally Compatible Colleges list and determine the type of college that is more compatible with your personal style. The "Best College Match" type that is most compatible for me would be most like

Admissions & Scholarships 101: "The Admissions Game"
Gaining admission and winning scholarships is a narrowing process on the part of the committees that make the decisions.
The process comes in two parts. The first of which is the basic _____ qualifier where based on your personal academic competencies and performance your application is further reviewed as a possibility or removed as being under qualified.

The four most widely used criteria to assess an applicant's basic qualifications are:

1. _____ .
2. _____ .
3. _____ .
4. _____ .

Although most of the application decision is made based on your Academic Profile, decision committees try to learn more about the applicant by looking deeper into their application particularly when an applicant is of interest and/or a borderline case.

How Do Colleges & Scholarships Use Our Applications?

How do they come to a decision to make a judgment about you?

This is done through the other important part of your overall application package that contains more subjective information about your:

1. _____
2. _____
3. _____
4. _____

These things should be well documented through the inclusion of your essays, letters of recommendations, class rank, extracurricular activities, special talents and skills, volunteerism, work history, travel history, interviews, awards and recognition.

Colleges and scholarship committees use all of this information _____ and _____ in deciding whether the applicant is the type of student who displays the personal character they desire.

Note: The 'tricky part' for the colleges and the applicants is that the colleges are primarily making their decisions based on objective information where their decisions are to a lesser degree 'tempered' by a varying degree of additional non-standard aforementioned information.

Extra Information Really Matters: If It Ever Sees the Light of Day

No one knows when or if their application will ever make it into true contention for admission or a scholarship award, but if you are going to submit an application:

If you're going to commit limited time then you must do quality work when completing the application process.

Your job as the applicant is to convey_____and_____using helpful pieces of information that_____and _____to enhance your overall application package.

The admissions and/or scholarship committees have to make a decision. It is your job to explain to them_____. Therefore, you must give the information provided in additional documents to explain clearly and concisely who you are and how choosing you would be a true _____ for you and them.

If you've done your college selection homework using the "Best College Match" process to prepare, your story should be _____, _____ and _____.

Character Always Counts

There's no substitute for a great story. So, if you want to find your "Best College Match" you have to do two things:

1. Make serious applications to the right types of colleges & scholarships based on your personal_____.
2. Get your great story supported by strong additional documentation_____ _____ by those making the approval decisions.

Don't Miss This!

Far too many otherwise strong applications are unsuccessful in gaining admissions or winning funding because they are submitted to colleges and scholarships that are not their "Best College Match".

Make sure that you know 'why' you are applying to the colleges and for the scholarships. The admissions and awards committees want to know that information as well.

Gregory and Opal Dawson

Chapter 4 Carefully Procuring College Funding

Finding your "Best College Match" price is one of the most important components of realizing your "Best College Match". Therefore, when procuring your "Best College Match" price, apply to the colleges and scholarships where you have a strong Relative Competitive Record and a higher probability of admissions acceptance where

Price = _____ **+** _____ .

The reality is that like most college students you may need to obtain some form of outside funding to pay for your "Best College Match". Keep in mind that the funding may be from multiple sources. Although every student's financial situation is different, varying parts of 10 basic sources of college funding can be used to pay for your "Best College Match".

The 10 Sources of College Funding

At "Best College Match" we want to help every student obtain their "Best College Match" from the college funding sources that are:

1. _____
2. _____
3. _____

Because . . . ***All sources of college funding are not created equal.***

Literally, it "pays" to investigate the price of your "Best College Match" because the _____ and _____ of potential funding varies greatly and sadly much of that funding goes _____ every year.

Complete the 10 sources for college funding, in order, from highest overall benefit to least overall benefit.

Not all sources of college funds are _____ to all students and not every student is going to meet the _____ requirements for every source of funding, nor is every source going to be _____ feasible for every student.

1. _____ Scholarships – are largely available from many sources and come in varying amounts most of which can be used at any given college.
2. _____ Scholarships – are institutional and can range from very small amounts to the proverbial "full-ride" although they are not portable if it's at a school that is a good fit they can be a great match.
3. _____ Aid – many colleges offer financial assistance packages to students depending on its recruitment focus. Work study on campus jobs would be an example.
4. _____ Scholarships – special talents and skills such as music, arts, debate or athletics offer limited scholarship opportunities for those students with these extra-ordinary types of talent. They range from partial to full basis where these talents are an asset to the school program.
5. _____ Aid – such as Pell Grants and the Federal Supplemental Educational Opportunity Grants are awarded with dollar limits based on eligible family income guidelines and are not available to all students.
6. _____ Aid – varies by state and generally offer both merit and need based awards depending on individual state guidelines and award amounts.
7. _____ Internships – are a super way to gain real life practical career related work experience and earn income that can be used to support your college education. They are available to all students but are awarded on a competitive basis.

8. _____ Assistance – direct monetary assistance from family is a great source of college funding. Each family helps their college student financially where the amount of that support can vary.

9. _____ Employment – having a part time job to earn money to help support college-cost offers the opportunity to get a college education that otherwise might be missed.

10. _____ Loans – the reality is that these days the cost of college is so expensive that many – sometimes too many – students take out loans to pay for college when they shouldn't. Student loans should not be your first or only avenue to pay for college. But under the right circumstance and in the absolute least amount with a great plan of how to repay it quickly, student loans can be an additional source of college educational funding.

Your Personal College Funding Packages

When structuring your "Best Collage Match" funding package use the following "Best College Match" Price Template from the addendum to figure your personal Net College Cost. The Net College Cost consists of the _____ minus _____.

A "Zero" Net College Cost means that the college cost has been _____.
A "Negative" Net College Cost means that the college cost has been _____.
A "Positive" Net College Cost means that the college cost has been _____.

'Best College Match' Price Template

Student Name: _____

College / Scholarship: _____

College Cost

Tuition: $ _____
Room & Board: $ _____
Books & Supplies: $ _____
Fees: $ _____
Other: $ _____
Total College Cost: $ _____

College Funding Sources

Non-Institutional Scholarships: $ _____
Institutional Merit Scholarships: $ _____
Institutional Student Aid: $ _____
Extra / Athletic Scholarships: $ _____
Federal Student Aid: $ _____
State Student Aid: $ _____
Paid Internships: $ _____
Family / Personal Assistance: $ _____
Part Time Employment: $ _____
Student Loans: $ _____
Total College Funding: $ _____

Net College Price:
(Total Cost - Total Funding) $ _____

Step 1: Add Personal Information

1. Start by adding any direct _____ contributions for college.
2. Add your estimated or actual_____contributions if applicable.
3. Add how much you might_____contribute to your college expenses.
4. Apply for all _____that is available to you.

Step 2: Where The "Best Match Price" Is Made!

1. Research and apply to the _____Scholarships that you think are your "Best College Match" given your Relative Competitive Record and that you feel you could be successful. Add any awards earned to the Best College Match Price Template.

2. Make direct application for admissions, _____and_____to the colleges that you think based on your ability, talent and "Best College Match" that you feel you could have a competitive chance of being successful. Add any awards earned to the Best College Match Price Template.

3. Research and apply to schools and other entities that offer_____in your field of interest that you feel you could have a competitive chance to be successful. Add any awards earned to the Best College Match Price Template.

Step 3: When & Where It Makes Sense

1. Consider_____**ONLY** after all other college funding sources have been 100% exhausted and where the loan is only part of the larger college funding package. Student loans should never be a first option and avoided totally if at all possible. At the same time, in certain situations they can be a valuable part of your "Best College Match" price. Add any awards earned to the Best College Match Price Template.

The Four Types of College Funding Prices

Best College Match Price

Relative Competitive Record

	Lower	Higher
Great (Funding Awarded)	In Demand Price	Merit Price
Good (Funding Awarded)	Standard Price	High Demand Price

In-Demand Price goes to students with a _____ and_____. Students who fall into this area represent some type of "specialty" or exceptional talent where it could be for super star athletes, great artists, debaters or quite possibly a school who has a desire to be more diverse and offer additional funding awards for these student groups.

Merit Price goes to students with a _____ and _____.
Students who fall into this area represent students at a given college who are the best of the best scholarly students with the strongest Academic Profiles (i.e. your highest quality merit applicants) who are offered large scholarships and other strong award funding packages from the college for students who have a real proven desire to attend that school.

Standard Price goes to students with a _____ and _____.
Students who fall into this area represent the majority of students at a college who have an average Academic Profile that will be more typical of the student body.

High-Demand Price goes to student with a _____ and _____.
Students who fall into this area represent those who have a strong Academic Profile but are not being amply funded. This situation usually happens when great students apply to very high-demand premier or prestigious colleges. The demand far exceeds the supply and many students who are accepted may not always get the best funding awards because the demand is so high.

Note: Your personal "Best College Match" price will be more or less financially rewarded much like gaining college admissions acceptances where depending on your Relative Competitive Record as compared with the concurrent college or scholarship Application Profile applicant pool you are competing against.

Therefore, when it comes to procuring your "Best College Match" price if you've chosen to apply to your "Best College Match" fit colleges and scholarships as outlined in Chapter 3, your overall Relative Competitive Record will be as high or higher than most. This fact should make gaining higher "Best College Match" price packages more likely where the resulting awards should be at least good if not great.

Thus, the value of _____, _____ and _____ your Academic Profile to actualize your _____ and ultimate benefit is nearly as important as having a great academic record alone.

Chapter 5   Honestly Picking the Best College Match

Your "Best College Match" is obtained when you balance your "Best College Match" fit and your "Best College Match" funding packages where:

Best College Match = _____ + _____

Therefore, the combination of your "Best College Match" fits and your "Best College Match" prices – i.e., your _____ and the concurrent _____ would now represent your "Best College Match" college choices.

When picking your "Best College Match", your personal understanding of the _____ and what's ultimately best for the _____ should *drive* **your decision.**

Use the Best College Match College Choice Ranker to complete the steps to determine your "Best College Match" Colleges.

Best College Match College Choice Ranker

BCM - Colleges Acceptance / Scholarship	Net College Cost	BCM Profile Type	Choice Rank
_____	_____	_____	_____
_____	_____	_____	_____
_____	_____	_____	_____
_____	_____	_____	_____
_____	_____	_____	_____
_____	_____	_____	_____
_____	_____	_____	_____
_____	_____	_____	_____
_____	_____	_____	_____
_____	_____	_____	_____

1. Complete the ranker with all the information requested including the BCM Profile Type information.

2. Based on what you now know and have achieved, and after completing the "Best College Match" process, rank your possible choices on your ranker in descending order.

3. As the "New You," personally review your choices for "Best College Match," and if necessary, seek further consultation to help you with your decision.

4. Pick the "Best College Match" offer that is the best overall fit and price for "YOU"!

Congratulations, you've chosen your own personal *"Best College Match".*

Gregory and Opal Dawson

Chapter 6 Addendum Contents

BCM Application Requirements and Deadlines	46
BCM Price Template	47
BCM Admission and Scholarship Basic Information	48
BCM Home Team Documentation	49
BCM Parental / Guardian Information	50
BCM Letters of Recommendation Information	51
BCM Extra-Curricular, Community Service, Employment & Volunteer Activities	52
BCM Awards, Honors & Recognitions	53
BCM Student Resume Template	54
BCM Student Profile Document	55
BCM Financial Aid Document	56
BCM Essay Manager	57
BCM Personal Photo File	58
BCM Envelope System	59
BCM I've Got It File	60

BCM Application Requirements and Deadlines

Admission / Scholarship: _____

Application Deadline: _____

Application Requirements	Requested	Completed
Application	_____	_____
Tour Completed	_____	_____
High School Transcripts	_____	_____
ACT / SAT Scores	_____	_____
Letters of Recommendation(s)	_____	_____
Extracurricular Information	_____	_____
Awards & Honors	_____	_____
Resume	_____	_____
School Profile	_____	_____
Financial Aid Information	_____	_____
Essay(s)	_____	_____
Personal Photo	_____	_____
Pre-Paid Envelopes	_____	_____
Other	_____	_____

Submitted On: _____

Application Status: _____

Approved / Declined: _____

'Best College Match' Price Template

Student Name: _____

College / Scholarship: _____

College Cost

Tuition: $ _____
Room & Board: $ _____
Books & Supplies: $ _____
Fees: $ _____
Other: $ _____
Total College Cost: $ _____

College Funding Sources

Non-Institutional Scholarships: $ _____
Institutional Merit Scholarships: $ _____
Institutional Student Aid: $ _____
Extra / Athletic Scholarships: $ _____
Federal Student Aid: $ _____
State Student Aid: $ _____
Paid Internships: $ _____
Family / Personal Assistance: $ _____
Part Time Employment: $ _____
Student Loans: $ _____
Total College Funding: $ _____

Net College Price:
(Total Cost - Total Funding) $ _____

Gregory and Opal Dawson

BCM Admissions & Scholarship Basic Information Documentation

* High School Transcript (supplied by student)

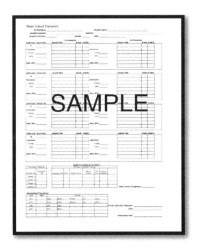

* ACT / SAT scores (supplied by student)

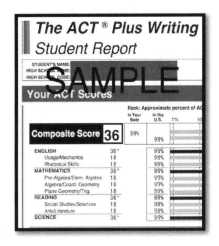

BCM- Home Team Documentation

Student Name: _____

Parent / Guardian: _____

School Support

Teacher	email	_____	phone	_____
Counselor	email	_____	phone	_____
Principal	email	_____	phone	_____
Coach	email	_____	phone	_____

Non School Support

Program Director	email	_____	phone	_____
Non Profit	email	_____	phone	_____
Extra Curricular	email	_____	phone	_____
Church	email	_____	phone	_____
Mentor	email	_____	phone	_____
College Rep	email	_____	phone	_____
Alumni / Group	email	_____	phone	_____

Peer To Peer Support / "The Buddy System"

BCM student participants	email	_____	phone	_____
Classmates	email	_____	phone	_____

Parental / Guardian Information

Name: _____

Relationship: _____

Mailing Address: _____

Home Phone: _____

Cell Phone: _____

Email Address: _____

Name: _____

Relationship: _____

Mailing Address: _____

Home Phone: _____

Cell Phone: _____

Email Address: _____

College Legacy Information

Name: _____

Relationship: _____

Year Graduated: _____

BCM – Letters of Recommendation Information

Recommendation For (Name): _____

Recommender: _____

Requested On: _____

Supporting documentation supplied to recommender on: _____

    1. Resume   _____
    2. Pre-Made & Paid Envelope   _____
    3. Requested Deadline Date of   _____
    4. Specific About the Request   _____

Actual Deadline Date: _____

Completed & Submitted On: _____

BCM - Extracurricular, Community Service, Employment & Volunteer Activities

Strategy: List all of your extracurricular, community service, employment and volunteer activities. Rank them from highest to lowest order of importance and record them in the table below.

Date(s)	Activities, Community Service and Employment / Position	Hrs / Wk
Example: Sep '14 - Present	Winning High School Debate Team, Team Captain	17

BCM - Awards, Honors & Recognitions

Strategy: List all of your awards, honors, and recognitions. Rank them from highest to lowest order of importance and record them below.

Scope*	Awards / Honors	Grade	Date
_____	_____	_____	_____
_____	_____	_____	_____
_____	_____	_____	_____
_____	_____	_____	_____
_____	_____	_____	_____
_____	_____	_____	_____
_____	_____	_____	_____
_____	_____	_____	_____
_____	_____	_____	_____
_____	_____	_____	_____
_____	_____	_____	_____
_____	_____	_____	_____
_____	_____	_____	_____
_____	_____	_____	_____
_____	_____	_____	_____

Scope* e.g. International, National, Regional, State, Local School

BCM – Student Resume Template

Use the BCM Extracurricular and Awards Templates to complete your resume.

(Name Here)   _____

Future Educational Goals:

Current Educational Status:

Awards & Recognitions:

Extracurricular Activities:

Work Experience / Volunteer Service:

Personal Interests:

Best College Match Workbook

BCM - School Profile Document

Many colleges and scholarships will require that a copy of your high school's "School Profile" be submitted as an application requirement from either you or from the school directly.

Request a copy from your counselor and keep it on hand for when it may be needed.

(Add School Profile here)

BCM - Financial Aid Documentation

All colleges and some scholarships will require financial information directly related to the amount of "Financial Aid" available to their student applicants and will ask for the below forms as verification.

1 FAFSA   Free Application for Federal Student Aid

2 SAR   Student Aid Report

3 CSS   CSS / Financial Aid PROFILE
                 (sometimes specifically requested by colleges)

BCM – Essay Manager

Essay For (Name): _____

Prompt: _____

Word Limit: _____

Started On: _____

Due By: _____

Reviewed Last On Date(s): _____

Completed On: _____

Essay For (Name): _____

Prompt: _____

Word Limit: _____

Started On: _____

Due By: _____

Reviewed Last On Date(s): _____

Completed On: _____

BCM Personal Photo File

Many colleges and or scholarships will ask its applicants for a personal photo in the form of either a small printed picture or a JPEG file as part of their application requirements.

It's a great idea to keep them both on hand just in case.

(Add your personal photos here)

BCM Envelope System

	Recommender	College / Scholarship	Date Due	Date Out
1	_____	_____	_____	_____
2	_____	_____	_____	_____
3	_____	_____	_____	_____
4	_____	_____	_____	_____
5	_____	_____	_____	_____
6	_____	_____	_____	_____
7	_____	_____	_____	_____
8	_____	_____	_____	_____
9	_____	_____	_____	_____
10	_____	_____	_____	_____

BCM - I got It, I Got It, I Got It Documentation File

(general file for extra just in case documentation, notes etc.)

List of Items in my BCM general information "catch-all" file

1 _____

2 _____

3 _____

4 _____

5 _____

6 _____

7 _____

8 _____

9 _____

10 _____

Made in the USA
Lexington, KY
15 September 2017